This Little Explore The book belongs to:

_____

For
Curious Learners

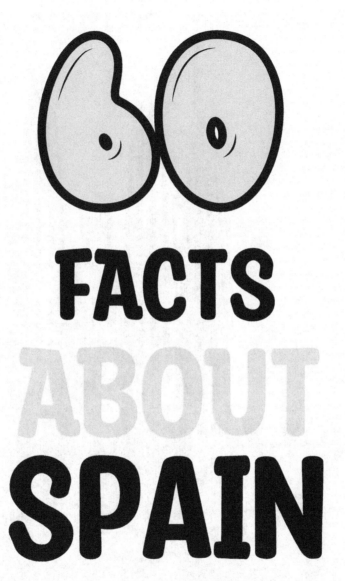

FACTS
ABOUT
SPAIN

60 Facts About Spain

Hola, little explorers! Do you love learning about faraway places and cool facts? Well, have you heard about a land full of flamenco music, vibrant cities, and mouth-watering paella? It's called Spain, and it's one of the most amazing countries in the world!

If you want to know more about Spain and its wonders, there's a super fun book you gotta check out. It's packed with interesting facts that are easy to devour, like tasty tapas, and it's got the most stunning photos you've ever seen! So grab a comfortable seat and get ready to embark on a journey to Spain through the pages of this book!

For Parents

We know that reading a book about a new country can be an exciting adventure for your child. It's important to remember that kids need breaks, and may not want to read the book all in one sitting. Encourage them to take breaks as needed, and ask them questions about what they've learned so far. Discussing the facts with your child can help them remember and retain the information better. You can also use the book as a springboard for further exploration and learning about Spain. Perhaps you can plan a family outing to try some Spanish food or visit a local museum with exhibits on ancient Spanish culture. Above all, we hope that this book sparks your child's curiosity and inspires them to learn more about the world around them.

MAP

The Facts

1. Spain is a country in the continent of Europe!

DID YOU KNOW?

2. Spain is located in southwestern Europe.

EUROPE IS THE SECOND-SMALLEST CONTINENT IN TERMS OF LAND AREA, COVERING ONLY ABOUT 10.18 MILLION SQUARE KILOMETRES, WHICH IS ROUGHLY 2% OF THE EARTH'S SURFACE. DESPITE ITS SMALL SIZE, EUROPE IS THE THIRD-MOST POPULOUS CONTINENT

3. Spain is bordered by France, Portugal, and Andorra.

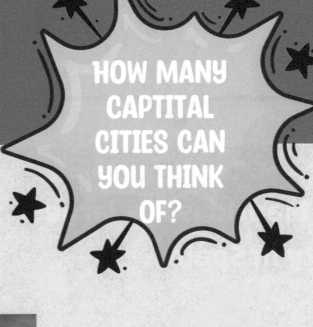

HOW MANY CAPTITAL CITIES CAN YOU THINK OF?

4. Madrid is the capital of Spain.

Pictured Palazzo de Cibeles

5. Spain is the fourth largest country in Europe.

Pictured The Cathedral of Madrid

6. Madrid is the largest city in Spain.

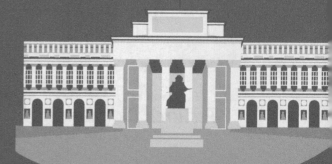

7. Spain is divided into 17 autonomous regions.

Pictured Plaza de Espana, Seville

8. The official language of Spain is Spanish.

Sound out these phrases

Hola - oh-lah (Hello)
Adiós - ah-dee-ohs (Goodbye)
Por favor - pohr fah-vohr (Please)
Gracias - grah-see-ahs (Thank you)

9. Spain has a population of over 47 million people.

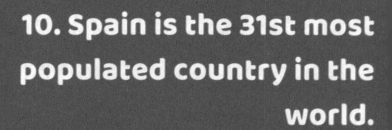

The Spanish national anthem, "La Marcha Real," is one of the few national anthems in the world that has no lyrics.

10. Spain is the 31st most populated country in the world.

11. Spain is a member state of the European Union.

The European Union (EU) is a political and economic union of 27 member states located in Europe. The EU was established by the Treaty of Maastricht in 1993 with the goal of promoting peace, stability, and economic prosperity in Europe.

12. The most popular sport in Spain is football.

13. Spain is known for its warm climate and beautiful beaches.

Pictured Gran Canarias

14. People from Spain are called Spanish.

15. Spain has over 8,000 kilometres of coastline.

16. The currency is the Euro.

17. The Spanish flag is called the "Rojigualda," which means "red-welded" in Spanish.

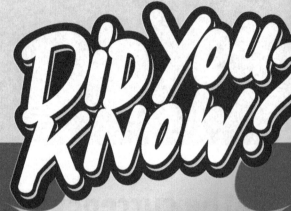

The current design of the flag was adopted on December 6, 1978, when the Spanish Constitution was approved.

18. The flag is made up of three horizontal stripes - red, yellow, and red.

19. The Spanish Armada was defeated by England in 1588.

Pictured Spanish Armada

Bullfighting, also known as corrida de toros, is a controversial traditional spectacle in Spain that dates back to the Roman Empire.

20. The national symbol of Spain is the bull.

21. The Plaza de Toros in Madrid is one of the most famous bullfighting arenas in the world.

Pictured Plaza de Toros

22. The Picos de Europa mountain range is located in northern Spain.

While some Spaniards view bullfighting as an important part of their culture and tradition, others oppose it and advocate for its abolition due to animal welfare concerns.

23. Spain is home to several famous festivals, including La Tomatina and Las Fallas.

24. La Tomatina is a festival held in Buñol, Valencia where participants throw overripe tomatoes at each other for fun.

25. The traditional Spanish dish paella originated in Valencia and typically contains rice, saffron, vegetables, and seafood or meat.

26. The national dish of Spain is paella.

HOW TO MAKE PAELLA FOR KIDS

1. Heat the olive oil in a large skillet or paella pan over medium heat.
2. Add the onion, red pepper, and garlic and sauté for 5 minutes, until the vegetables are soft.
3. Stir in the rice, paprika, salt, and black pepper and cook for 1-2 minutes, stirring constantly.
4. Pour in the chicken or vegetable broth and bring to a boil. Reduce the heat to low and simmer for 20-25 minutes, or until the rice is cooked through and the liquid has been absorbed.
5. Add the cooked shrimp, chicken, and frozen peas and cook for an additional 5-10 minutes, until everything is heated through.
6. Serve and enjoy your delicious paella!

27. The Royal Palace of Madrid is the largest royal palace in Western Europe.

The Royal Palace of Madrid is not used as a residence by the Spanish royal family, but rather for state ceremonies and official functions.

28. The Park Güell in Barcelona, designed by Antoni Gaudí, features colorful mosaics and whimsical architecture.

29. The third longest river in the Iberian Peninsula, the Tagus, flows through Spain.

Pictured Leon San Isidoro Church

30. Christianity is largest religion in Spain.

Religion in Spain is dominated by the Catholic Church.

Pictured The Bielsa Church

31. The Sagrada Familia in Barcelona is an unfinished church designed by Antoni Gaudí that has been under construction for over 135 years.

32. The construction on the Sagrada Familia began in 1882 and is still ongoing to this day, with an estimated completion date of 2026.

33. Spanish is one of the most spoken languages in the world.

34. Spain has the highest number of bars per capita in the world.

DID YOU KNOW?

Spanish is the official language in 21 countries, including Spain, Mexico, Colombia, Argentina, and Peru.

35. The Costa del Sol is a popular tourist destination on the southern coast of Spain.

Pictured Marbella, Costa del sol

Costa del Sol is a popular coastal region in the southern part of Spain. The name "Costa del Sol" means "Coast of the Sun" in Spanish, and it's easy to see why with its sunny weather almost all year round.

36. The city of Granada is famous for the Alhambra palace and its beautiful gardens.

37. Spain is the second-largest producer of wine in the world, after Italy.

38. The oldest university in Spain, the University of Salamanca, was founded in 1218.

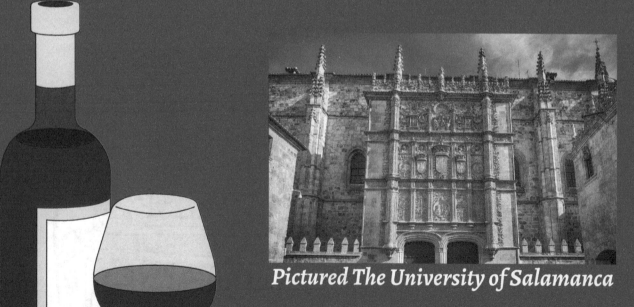

Pictured The University of Salamanca

39. Spain has won the FIFA World Cup once, in 2010.

DID YOU KNOW?

The Spanish national football team has also won multiple international titles, including the World Cup and the UEFA European Championship.

40. Spain is home to two of the world's best-known football clubs, Real Madrid and FC Barcelona.

41. Spain has a long history of Moorish influence, which is reflected in its architecture and cuisine.

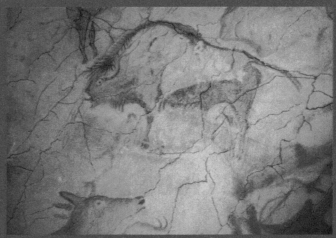

42. The Cave of Altamira in Cantabria is famous for its prehistoric cave paintings.

Pictured The Cave of Altamira

43. Native animals of Spain include brown bears, wolves, lynx, goats and donkeys.

44. Spain is home to a diverse range of wildlife, including a variety of mammals, birds, reptiles, and marine animals.

45. Spain has the largest population of registered donkeys in the European Union.

46. The largest number of wind turbines in the world can be found in Spain.

47. Spain is one of the most-visited countries in the world.

48. In Spain, it is tradition to eat a dozen grapes as the clock strikes midnight on the new year.

49. The Ebro is the longest river that is wholly in Spain and the second longest in the Iberian Peninsula.

50. Europe's only desert is in Spain. The desert is located in Almeria and is called Tabernas Desert.

51. Many people in Spain have a long rest in the afternoon called a 'Siesta'.

52. Spain is the home of some of the world's greatest artists such as Diego Veláques, Francisco Goya, El Greco, Pablo Picasso and Salvador Dali.

Pablo Picasso was a famous Spanish artist born on October 25, 1881. He is known for his innovative and influential paintings, including "Les Demoiselles d'Avignon" and "Guernica".

53. Popular dishes in Spain include fabada, pulpo a la gallega, pisto, gazpacho, tortilla and croquetas.

54. In Spain, many people eat doughnuts (churros) and chocolate for breakfast.

55. Spain is famous for Flamenco dance style.

56. Many people in Spain have two surnames; the first is the father's surname and the second is the mother's.

57. At around 320 million, Spain is home to the most Olive Trees in the world.

58. Spain's Mediterranean climate allows for the growth of citrus fruits, nuts, olives and grapes.

Did You Know?

The oldest known olive tree in Spain is the "Olivo de Fuentebuena" in Jaén, estimated to be between 1,200 and 2,000 years old.

59. The Camino de Santiago, or Way of St. James, is a popular pilgrimage route in Spain that ends at the Cathedral of Santiago de Compostela in Galicia.

60. The Spanish Civil War took place from 1936-1939.

Places To Go

Places To Go

Are you ready to go on an adventure to Spain? Get your passports ready, grab your camera, and let's explore the most amazing places in Spain! From the ancient buildings of the Madrid to the stunning beaches of Malaga, we'll discover the treasures of this beautiful country. Get ready to learn about the myths and legends that surround these magical places.

So come on, let's pack our bags and get ready to embark on an unforgettable journey to Spain!

Barcelona - This vibrant city is located in the northeast region of Spain and is known for its stunning architecture, delicious food, and bustling nightlife.

Madrid - The capital of Spain, Madrid is a hub of culture and history. Visitors can enjoy the Prado Museum, the Royal Palace, and the lively Plaza Mayor.

Seville - Located in the southern region of Andalusia, Seville is known for its stunning architecture, rich history, and vibrant flamenco music and dance scene.

Granada - This beautiful city in southern Spain is known for its rich history, stunning architecture, and the famous Alhambra Palace.

Salamanca: A UNESCO World Heritage Site known for its stunning Plaza Mayor and the historic University of Salamanca, one of the oldest universities in the world.

Toledo: A medieval walled city with a rich history, known for its stunning Gothic cathedral, Alcázar fortress, and labyrinthine streets.

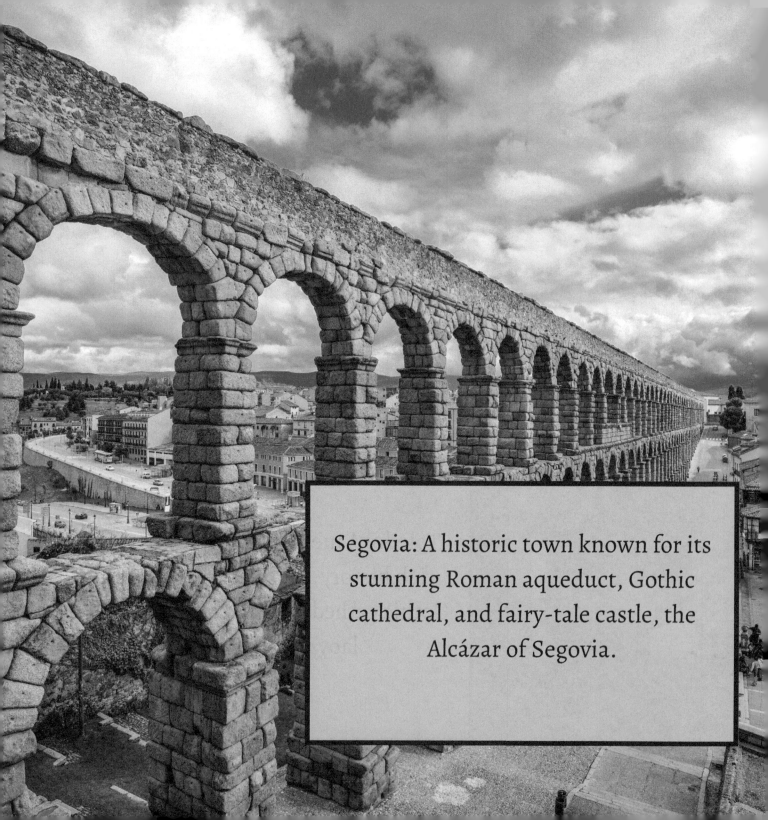

Segovia: A historic town known for its stunning Roman aqueduct, Gothic cathedral, and fairy-tale castle, the Alcázar of Segovia.

San Sebastian: A picturesque coastal city in the Basque Country known for its stunning beaches, world-class cuisine, and lively cultural scene.

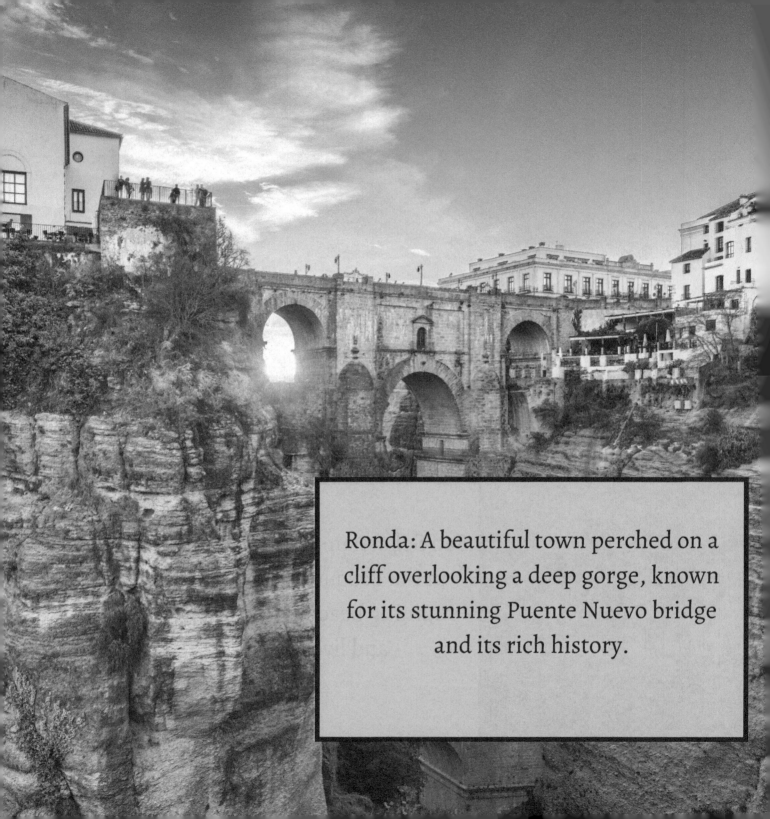

Ronda: A beautiful town perched on a cliff overlooking a deep gorge, known for its stunning Puente Nuevo bridge and its rich history.

Bilbao: A modern and vibrant city in the Basque Country, home to the famous Guggenheim Museum Bilbao and the historic Casco Viejo district.

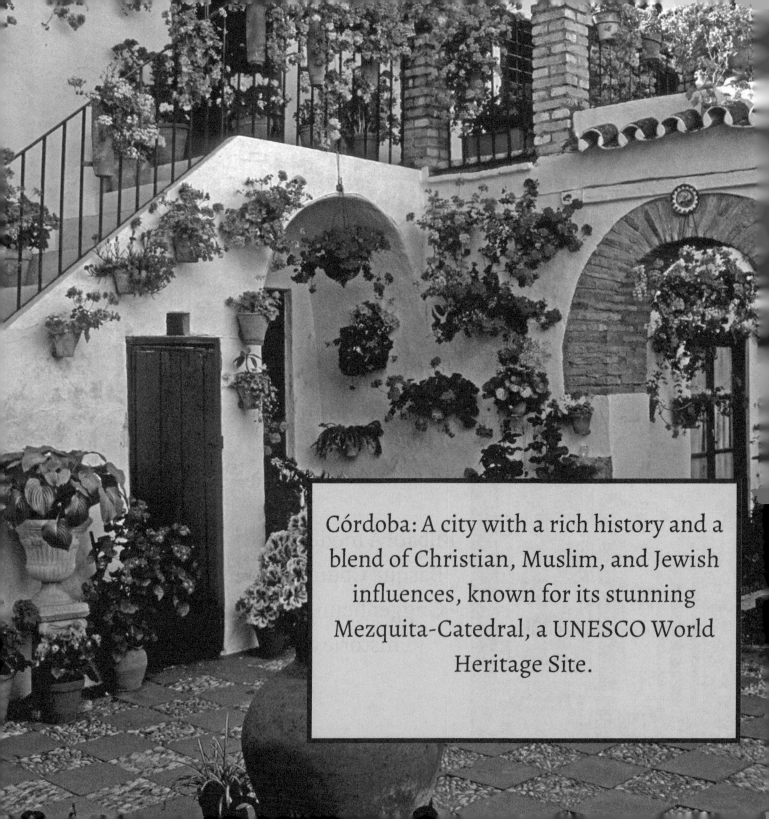

Córdoba: A city with a rich history and a blend of Christian, Muslim, and Jewish influences, known for its stunning Mezquita-Catedral, a UNESCO World Heritage Site.

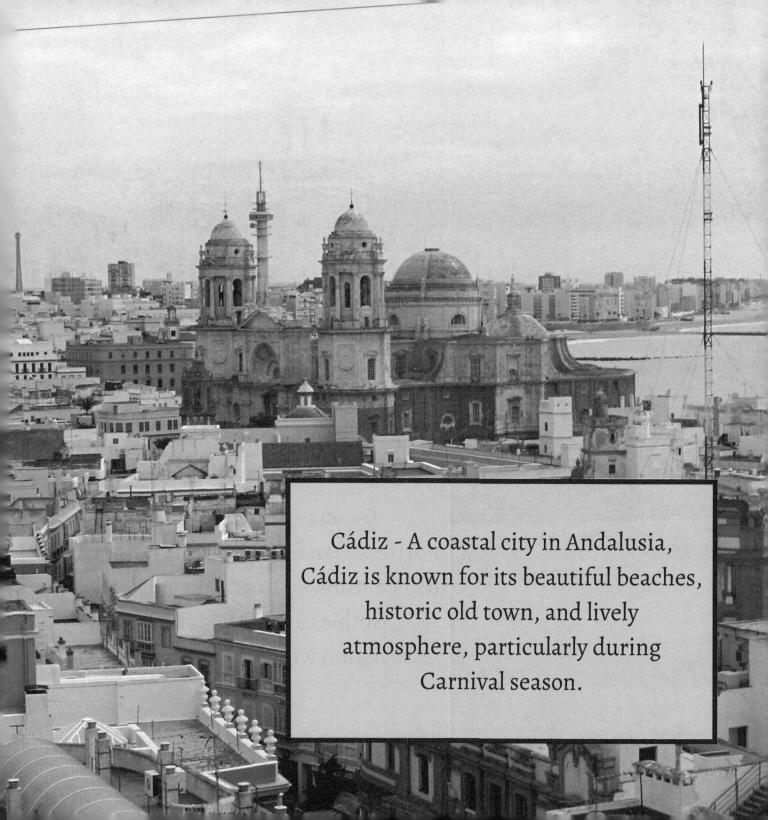

Cádiz - A coastal city in Andalusia, Cádiz is known for its beautiful beaches, historic old town, and lively atmosphere, particularly during Carnival season.

Girona - A medieval town in northeastern Spain, Girona is known for its beautiful old town, ancient walls, and Gothic cathedral, as well as its association with the TV series "Game of Thrones".

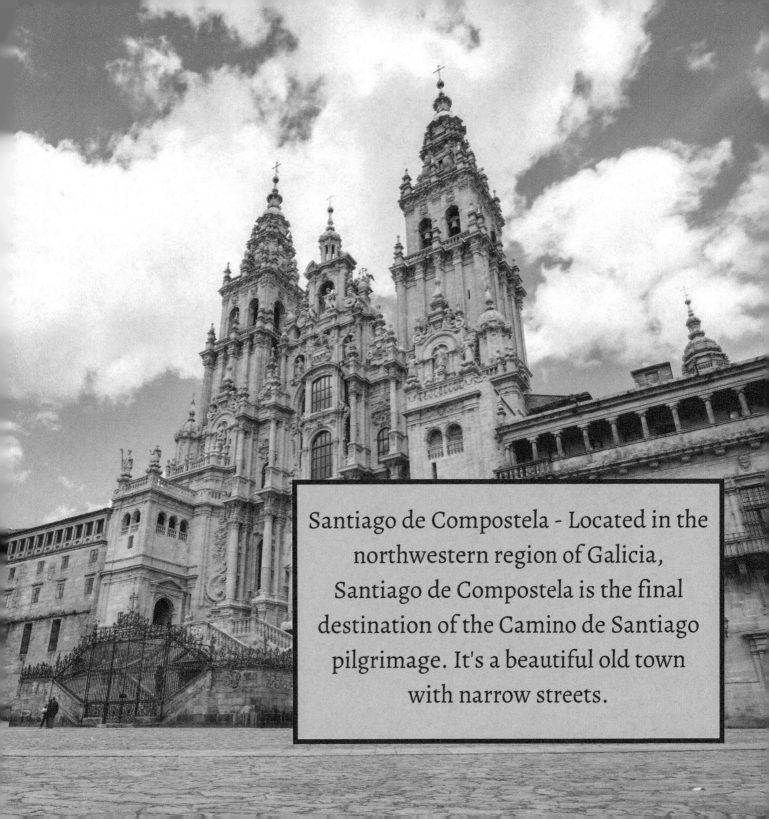

Santiago de Compostela - Located in the northwestern region of Galicia, Santiago de Compostela is the final destination of the Camino de Santiago pilgrimage. It's a beautiful old town with narrow streets.

Explore

Explore

The "Explore?" section is a fun way to test your knowledge about Spain. You can answer trivia questions about the country, its history, culture, and traditions. See how many you can get right and challenge your friends and family to see who knows the most. Don't worry if you don't know the answer to every question, because you can always learn something new by reading this book again and exploring more about Spain. Have fun!

Test Yourself

What is the capital city of Spain?
Answer: Madrid.

What famous building in Barcelona was designed by the architect
Antoni Gaudi?
Answer: The Sagrada Familia.

What is the name of the famous Spanish dish that includes rice,
seafood, and vegetables?
Answer: Paella.

What is the name of the Spanish dance where people stomp their
feet and clap their hands?
Answer: Flamenco.

Test Yourself

What is the name of the famous soccer team from Barcelona?
Answer: FC Barcelona.

What is the name of the Spanish king?
Answer: King Felipe VI.

What is the name of the Spanish language?
Answer: Spanish, also known as Castilian.

What famous artist was from Spain and painted pictures with melting clocks?
Answer: Salvador Dali.

What is the name of the famous running of the bulls festival in Pamplona?
Answer: The San Fermin festival.

Activities To Try

Activities

Welcome to the Activities section! Here, you'll find a variety of fun and engaging activities related to Spain. Each activity is designed to help you explore different aspects of Spanish culture and history in a hands-on way. Whether you want to create your own Spanish fan, try some traditional Spanish foods, or learn some Spanish dances, we've got you covered.

We encourage you to try out as many of these activities as you like, and don't be afraid to put your own spin on them. Use your creativity and imagination to make them your own! So, get ready to have some fun and learn about Spain in a new way.

Make a Spanish fan

Materials needed:
Popsicle sticks or wooden skewers
Coloured tissue paper
Glue

Instructions:
1. Cut the tissue paper into strips.
2. Glue one end of the tissue paper to the top of the popsicle stick.
3. Fold the tissue paper over the stick and glue the other end of the tissue paper to the bottom of the stick.
4. Continue gluing the tissue paper to the stick, alternating colours until you reach the end of the stick.
5. Once you have finished, hold the fan by the bottom stick and fan it open to reveal the beautiful colours.

Make a Spanish flag

Materials needed:

White construction paper

Red and yellow paint

Paintbrushes

Instructions:

1. Draw a rectangle shape on the white construction paper with a pencil.
2. Paint the top half of the rectangle red and the bottom half yellow.
3. Let the paint dry completely.
4. Once the paint is dry, wave your flag proudly.

Learn to count in Spanish

Materials needed:

Paper

Pencil

Instructions:

1. Write the numbers 1-10 in Spanish on a piece of paper.
2. Say each number out loud and practice counting with your child.
3. Challenge your child to count objects around the house in Spanish.

Make a Spanish Omelette (Tortilla de Patatas)

Materials needed:

Potatoes

Eggs

Onion

Olive oil

Salt

Instructions:

1. Peel and chop the potatoes into small cubes.
2. Peel and chop the onion into small pieces.
3. Heat the olive oil in a frying pan over medium heat.
4. Add the potatoes and onion to the pan and fry until the potatoes are golden brown.
5. In a bowl, whisk together the eggs and a pinch of salt.
6. Add the fried potatoes and onion to the bowl with the eggs and stir to combine.
7. Heat a little more oil in the pan and pour the egg mixture into the pan.
8. Cook for a few minutes until the bottom of the omelette is set.
9. Carefully flip the omelette over and cook until the other side is set.
10. Serve the omelette hot and enjoy!

Flamenco Dancing

Materials needed:

Flamenco music

Scarves or shawls

Instructions:

1.   Put on some Flamenco music.
2.   Hold a scarf or shawl in each hand and follow the beat of the music.
3.   Move your feet and hips in time with the music.
4. Practice some Flamenco arm movements by holding one arm up and the other down, and then switching.
5.   You can even dress up in traditional Flamenco clothing to get in the spirit!

The most important part of this activity is having fun and moving

Glossary

Glossary

Barcelona: A city in northeastern Spain, famous for its art and architecture.

Bullfighting: A traditional Spanish sport where a person fights a bull in an arena.

Costa del Sol: A coastal region in southern Spain known for its sunny weather and beaches.

Flamenco: A style of music and dance that originated in southern Spain.

La Sagrada Familia: A famous cathedral in Barcelona that has been under construction since 1882.

Madrid: The capital city of Spain, known for its art museums and beautiful architecture.

Olive trees: A common tree in Spain, known for producing olives that are used to make olive oil.

Pablo Picasso: A famous Spanish artist born in 1881, known for his paintings and sculptures.

Paella: A traditional Spanish rice dish, usually made with seafood or chicken and vegetables.

Royal Palace of Madrid: A beautiful palace in the centre of Madrid that is the official residence of the Spanish royal family.

Spanish football: A popular sport in Spain, with famous teams like Real Madrid and FC Barcelona.

Author's Note

Dear young readers,

I am so excited to have shared with you all about Spain, a country that is rich in history, art, mythology, and culture. As an author, I am always inspired by the incredible diversity and beauty of the world around us, and I hope this book has inspired you to explore and learn more about Spain.

I was inspired to write this book because I believe that learning about different cultures and countries can help us understand and appreciate the world better. It's so important to celebrate and learn from different traditions and ways of life, and I hope this book has helped you do just that.

If you enjoyed reading this book, I would love it if you could leave a review on Amazon. Reviews help other readers discover the book and can make a big difference for independent authors like myself.
Thank you for joining me on this journey, and I hope this book has sparked your curiosity and imagination. Keep exploring and learning about the world around you!

Sincerely,
Grant Publishing

Made in United States
Orlando, FL
11 October 2024

52549095R00043